Abandoned Japan

Jordy Meow

Introduction

Haikyo simply means "ruin" in Japanese. But haikyo also describes the Japanese version of the hobby known as urban exploration. Haikyoists, as we call them, visit abandoned towns, houses, hospitals, schools, industrial sites, theme parks and virtually any forgotten or abandoned place.

The ruins they explore in Japan aren't the result of disasters such as the tsunami or earthquakes. Dark tourism – exploration based on tragedy – is not considered appropriate by most haikyoists. Haikyo are from the remnants of the mining industry, the industrial revolution, the exodus to the city after World War II, the burst of the financial bubble during the '90s and the decadent demography of Japan. Through photos, memories and stories, the haikyoists keep the past alive and make us more conscious about what tomorrow could be.

Those who cannot remember the past are condemned to repeat it.
Spanish philosopher George Santayana

A striking aspect of haikyo (especially in comparison with Western urban exploration) is that the places are usually in a very good state of repair. The haikyo community has a strong desire to respect and keep the ruins as they are, whereas most Japanese people stay away altogether. More than anywhere else in the world the urban explorers' famous motto is respected: take nothing but pictures, leave nothing but footprints. Also, to protect the places, most of them are kept secret and labelled with the first letter of the area name (city or prefecture) followed by the place type. We therefore have many S医院 (Clinic S) or F学校 (School F) which makes it virtually impossible to find the location from its name. Also, the pictures themselves are taken in a way that avoids giving any clue to the location. So it's common for explorers to carry out some kind of triangulation based on features and details (topographic, historical, factual) in the photos. If the place is relatively well known, things become a little easier and looking up old documents helps to finally pinpoint the location.

Haikyo can be found easily while driving or even by checking maps in advance. Looking for places is an extremely fun part of *haikyo* but finding them alone is even better, especially when they've never been documented before.

One of the best aspects of *haikyo* is the community. This community has existed for a long time but it has been growing exponentially with the rise of social media networks and the affordability of photography. It consists of many social groups or even teams. I started *haikyo* with my colleagues and friends. Then I joined people who seemed, at first, the most prominent actors on the scene; a first layer with a better presence online. But over time I became close friends with *haikyoists* from the deeper communities and quickly found a hobby that was enjoyed in a different way. They have a very strong respect for the ruins, working on discovering, protecting and even cleaning them. They dislike seeing *haikyo* used as a background for post-apocalyptic scenes. In short, they're not using the ruins for themselves. The ruins become part of their life; new members of their alternative family. This *haikyo* community, with their very unique approach, had a real impact on me. I cannot claim to have become one of them but I still like the dramatic dimension of the ruins without getting too attached emotionally.

The world around is filled with colours and rays of light with which these abandoned places are vibrant. Ghostly shadows and colours jump out everywhere. *Haikyo* seem so silent at first but when you are accustomed to them you start hearing nature all around. There are always birds singing among other odd noises and, sometimes, those huge Japanese frogs make your heart jump. And the smells: the grass, the old wood, or the scent of old paper. Sometimes a place turns out to be really dark and humid, deadly and nightmarish. In such cases I try to add a flicker of light myself, hoping to infuse some life into it. There's always something worthwhile to experience. I try my best to convey my feelings while visiting a *haikyo* in the photographs. I hope you'll feel as if you're discovering these places as you turn the pages of this book.

Content

Towns

Many people think of Japan as a small overpopulated island but this isn't true. Of course, Tokyo and Osaka are swarming with people while Kyoto has to accommodate crowds of tourists. But the rest of Japan offers a completely different experience. The countryside, the heart of Japan, looks rather unpopulated.

The demographic issue isn't going to be resolved any time soon. Although the population is increasing in major Japanese cities, the overall population is falling. Young people, especially, are moving to urban areas in droves, mainly for educational, economic and cultural reasons. There are about 8 million vacant houses and apartments nationwide. Those areas are *genkai shuuraku*, meaning that they're "beyond the limit" because it seems as if nobody will come to reclaim the properties and the land.

Tokyo has been subjected to the most deadly bombing raids in history. Half of the city was wiped out during World War II. Other cities suffered air raids and even atomic bombs. Those cities were completely rebuilt and are continually being modernized in readiness for the 2020 Olympic Games. They now display Japanese popular culture with its *anime*, *manga* and J-pop trends, to name but a few. But the spirit of ancient Japan is cloistered in the countryside.

The Red Villa
赤別荘
1922–1980

Japan's remote villages are full of secrets and abandoned houses. In the Kanto area, wealthy families used to build houses with a Western look as if the country was a former colony. Today, those abandoned houses have a very particular aura and they have their share of tales to tell.

We found the Red Villa next to a lake in Ibaraki prefecture, surrounded by a wild bamboo grove. Looking through it, I had my first glimpse of this beautiful villa built in 1922.

We were welcomed by a creepy doll at the entrance and an antique phone. This was the ground floor, consisting of barely recognizable dining room and kitchen. There were a few TV sets, a sure sign that the family was quite a wealthy one. Multiple photos of themselves lie around, happily enjoying their life or posing for the camera. It seems to have been a large family, probably three generations living at the same place.

We went up and found the second floor even more interesting, with bedrooms and a nice balcony with a big comfy-looking chair, the ideal place for a nap.

But the real secret of this house was inside a very small room at the back of the main bedroom. Behind ripped black curtains we discovered a little laboratory. On the bottles lying around, we could read *Kodak Sodium Carbonate* and *Dry Plate* boxes next to them. A former darkroom!

There were many documents, letters written in English, developed prints and dry plates, which are like negatives. We took them over to the window and discovered many pictures of the house, family reunions, people playing together, not to mention some pornography. The resident photographer must have had fun experimenting with all these different styles.

The house became a *haikyo* in the '80s. I don't know why it was abandoned but I'm pretty certain that the clue is still inside the house, waiting for someone to discover it.

Sanno Village
山王
1889–1970s

We finally parked the car after driving along a winding mountain road. There was nothing much to see, only a few steps simply constructed from rocks leading up into the forest. We followed this path at first but a few minutes later the trail completely disappeared!

My fellow explorers switched on a serious-looking GPS because our mobile phones were longer picking up a signal. The village seemed to be a few kilometres farther into the forest. The mountainside was very steep and covered with fallen trees. This wasn't a relaxing Sunday stroll. The GPS device eventually lost the signal and it became difficult to find our bearings. There was no sign of any houses or even the old mountain track.

We decided to split up. Two of us headed for an area where the trees looked somehow thicker, as if they'd been cultivated, and that may have been the case as we came upon a levelled area with a little stone wall. The village wasn't far away.

Crumbling wooden houses, grass and trees covering everything, farming and forestry tools everywhere. The cemetery seemed to have taken over the whole village, with tombs scattered all over the place. There was also a temple slightly off to one side, from where there would once have been a good view of the village. It looked like some kind of wooden version of Angkor Wat, if not as elaborate or beautiful. But we'd found it: the old loggers' village.

Sanno was one of those villages that supplied the massive amounts of wood and charcoal needed for the construction of new towns and cities, but also for many wooden products (such as sake barrels). Then in 1960 timber imports were liberalized and cheap wood from abroad began to be shipped in. These villages couldn't survive and were gradually abandoned.

It's said that there were still a few people in the little village of Sanno in 1975.

Nichitsu Village
ニッチツ鉱山村

I've visited Nichitsu ghost town several times. It's easily accessible from Tokyo by car for a one-day trip and a worthwhile experience. I never fail to take friends interested in *haikyo* to Nichitsu.

The abandoned tin-mining village, about 50 km from Chichibu in Saitama, can also be reached from Kofu in Yamanashi. Apart from the detritus of the mining industry, the gloomy tunnels are an interesting sight. The best time to visit is probably autumn, with its profusion of magnificently coloured foliage.

Nichitsu is the name of the mining company that owns the village. The workers had to live on site because of the distance from the main cities. So the village grew in size until in its heyday it had as many as 3,000 residents. There were two schools, a clinic, a post office and even a cinema. The bosses lived in pleasant houses with tiled roofs and good exposure to the sun, whereas the ordinary workers' apartments along the riverside or on the cliff slopes had no bathrooms.

Sometime in the '80s, the once prosperous village was abandoned. It seems that a few of the buildings were used again in the '90s by young men – in the rooms of the most modern ones we found karaoke machines, *manga* books, piles of pornography, Gundam robot models and even a giant Pikachu.

Midori No Sono
みどりのその愛育園
1948–1992

Entering the ground of an abandoned property is always rather frightening. I dread discovering a dead body. Every year, a lot of deceased people are found in their home, sometimes even with the knowledge of relatives who are keeping them virtually alive to cash their pension. But others were just alone, forgotten, and died peacefully in their bed.

Before opening a door, my imagination always brings up a bloodcurdling image which I guess would help me to handle things better if there was indeed something there. I've had this feeling at Midori No Sono a few times.

Midori No Sono is more than a house, it was actually a small nursery run by a very kind woman. Past the entrance are two little buildings, both looking like private houses. The one on the right is very strange and seems to have a tree growing through it.

Upstairs was the most amazing experience though. It felt as if we'd just entered a Western house frozen in the mid '80s. The only Japanese element in this room was a cup of tea, the only token of life left after the owner passed away in 1992. Still half-full, the tea had thickened over time. I wonder if she looked at the reflection of her kind face one last time in this cup before leaving this world.

The House of Freedom
昭和初期の洋館H邸
1928–1972

A few years back, a *haikyoist* friend shared this location with me. He simply told me I should visit when I had the chance, adding that it had been a popular *haikyo* in the '90s when he'd explored it, without a camera. I looked for information and photos but found nothing, so I kept it on record but never checked it out.

Almost three years later, I found myself in front of a house with another explorer in Koga City, Ibaraki prefecture, not far from Tokyo. Stunned by the majestic appearance of this place, I realized that it was the place my friend had mentioned. And I learned a lesson: never avoid checking out a place because of lack of information.

The House of Freedom was massive and looked like a big block of concrete with little chimneys. It was surrounded by its own miniature jungle. We had to jump over a metal fence to get into the grounds, then find a path through the trees to reach the entrance.

The place was grand. Once past the concrete-built Meiji-era entrance, it looked more like a mixture of Edo and Western. Upstairs, a set of windows made an impressive play of light on the floor.

The design and architecture of this place was carefully thought out. There was even a swimming pool on the roof to make sure no comforts were lacking.

When the house was built in 1928 by Hachiro Hatsumi, a wealthy politician born in the city, this part of Ibaraki was mainly rice fields and there was no other place like it. He died two years later. Afterwards the house was supposed to be used for meetings of the Freedom and People's Rights Movement but it's difficult to be sure what happened.

There are many signs of family life and the house seems to have been inhabited until 1972, probably by members of the Hatsumi family as there's a photo of one of them in the dining room.

I went back a few years later only to discover that the house and been demolished and the site covered with solar panels. Hopefully this is for the best, but my heart is saddened.

Sento: Tsuru no Yu

鶴の湯
1923–2014

Sento are found everywhere in Japan, even in the cities. They are communal baths, originally used by people who didn't have a bathroom at home. There used to be over 2,000 *sento* in Tokyo. Their numbers grew especially after World War II, peaking in the '70s. Nowadays, they're still used by locals and appreciated as a way of connecting with the neighbourhood.

Strolling through Tokyo you can spot those *sento* by the black smoke streaming from their high chimneys. The water isn't from natural streams like that of the *onsen* spas, just ordinary water heated by a rudimentary coal boiler.

My friend Stéphanie is a *sento otaku*. She loves them and has visited every single one. Although she's French, she's become part of the Sento Committee in Tokyo. She took me to a few of them and pointed out that they always have their own unique art inside: paintings on the wall. Usually, traditional *sento* have a painting of Fuji-san with a few variations from one to another – perhaps a different viewpoint, different goings on in the foreground or a different season.

We also visited the Tsuru No Yu *sento*, which was closed, but the kindly owner opened the doors for us. The coal heating system had broken down a few years back and it would have cost millions of yen to repair, which unfortunately would not have been worthwhile; *sento* are today more a passion than a real business.

In a few years there'll be no real *sento* in Tokyo any more – another disappearing feature of Japanese culture. I wish they could be replaced with pretty little Japanese gardens featuring a few *sento* memories, but the odds are more and more in favour of shiny new high-rise buildings.

Yet a few modernized *sento* have learned how to survive, offering spa services such as mud baths, hammams, saunas, aromatherapy and even wine baths. Maybe this will help to keep a few original *sento* alive as well, as one or two are closing every week. As of 2015, there were about 600 of them left in Tokyo.

Seika Dormitory
精華寮
1927–2007

An authentic ruin made from reinforced concrete in the middle of Tokyo. Is that even possible? This dormitory built in 1927 as a foreign students' residence was used until recently, home to thirty-eight Taiwanese students. Tragically, on 20 July 2007 at 4.55 am, one of the residents fell asleep in his bed while smoking a cigarette. A few minutes later, the entire building caught fire. Two women were killed and seven other people were injured. Most of the room contents were reduced to ashes.

Difficult to imagine what the building looked like before the fire. From outside it was a lifeless and colourless bunker. Once inside, it reminded us of the court of Block 65 (an iconic building on the abandoned island of Gunkanjima – see p. 196). The ambiance was sad and painful. Many personal belongings were still lying around, some recognizable, some not.

After exploring the carbonized rooms I found a few in a better state. That was when I came across this letter, left on a table. The writer had a brain tumour and was living his last moments hoping to see a friend once more. Visiting the Seika Dormitory was rather an odd experience, somehow moving and dramatic at the same time.

Nakagin Capsule Tower
中銀カプセルタワー

Buildings in Tokyo are never really abandoned. They always have an owner who either stops maintaining them or avoids renewing tenants' leases. Building standards and anti-seismic technologies are always improving so there isn't much chance for old buildings. Cities seeking to attract rich property owners also want to get rid of those remnants of the past. Although there are more and more derelict buildings in Tokyo they don't usually survive long in the cityscape.

Luckily, Nakagin Capsule Tower hasn't been destroyed yet. Designed by Kishi Kurokawa in 1972, this building is the symbol of the Metabolism architectural movement popular after World War II. It's the first and last modular capsule apartment block to be built using the best features of that concept.

The capsules were prefabricated elsewhere, brought to Tokyo and attached to the main frame. They were supposed to slot in and out easily but this proved impractical, as in order to detach one capsule all those above would first have to be removed. The capsules aged and the building began to slide into disrepair. The massive usage of asbestos also left Nakagin unsafe to live in. As the building was threated with demolition, a number of architects reacted and bought the capsules independently in order to renovate them.

I became friendly with one of these architects: Maeda-san. He was at first intrigued by the mysterious-looking building and its unique interior and bought his first capsule back in 2010. He managed to make it into a habitable apartment despite problems such as a leaking roof. He's amused that so many people want to live there even though there are no hot showers! Luckily there's still a *sento* nearby and a single shower in the reception area.

Maeda-san added that he doesn't believe Nakagin will be demolished soon. The capsules are all being bought and restored and that should probably save it. Today, he's buying more capsules and enjoys being there, surrounded by a small but very interesting community of architects and artists. He's amazed that the building also attracts a lot of *haikyo* explorers. Some of the owners have listed their capsules for rent on Airbnb.

At one point, Nakagin was almost empty, filthy, dilapidated and facing demolition. But today the building has life, a community and a few lights are always on at night. The architects are trying their best to save it but its future remains uncertain.

The Royal House
Story from an Abandoned House in Hakone

華麗なる一族 廃墟
1948–1989

In the middle of the luxuriant woods of Kanagawa, we felt like Hansel and Gretel when we discovered this abandoned house. This one isn't made of gingerbread though. But maybe we'd discover an old witch and her stupendous stories? Here is the Royal House, one of the most famous *haikyo* in Japan. Known in Japanese as *Karei Naru Ichizoku* (A Majestic Family), its location has been kept secret for years to protect the precious artefacts it holds.

Trees have fallen on the house, destroying windows and part of the roof. Since then, damp has infiltrated everything: the wood of the main structure has become very spongy, and the plaster on the outside walls is covered with mould. But despite the decay, we can guess that this house has a rich past and entering will be like reading a story from an old book, the pages disintegrating into dust as we turn them.

The windows are all open so we can easily get in. A doll in a kimono welcomes us at the entrance. Yes, that's a traditional introduction to a *haikyo*!

The ground floor consists of a large dining room with a small kitchen behind. The dining room is an amazing discovery. Two ancient TV sets, lots of tiny antiques and a huge panda with a smashed skull. The kitchen is in a more precarious state than the rest. I try to walk across the floor but it suddenly subsides 50 cm. Too risky to go farther, though I'd love a peek into the refrigerator. There might be food with long-ago expiry dates and signs of a past life? I can just make out a third TV set in there: the first in the Sony Trinitron range, the KV-1310, a model dating from 1968.

We climb the stairs. The floor is fortunately more stable than I thought. Up there, two more rooms, filled with more treasures. At the entrance to the first, a picture of an old Japanese woman. Farther away, same size, another photo. This one depicts an old Westerner, a cigar in his fingers and a glass of wine in front of him. Did he live here with his Japanese wife?

I enter the first room, which looks like an office but it's difficult to see clearly. The forest around the house is so dense that, despite the three large windows, the rooms are still very dark.

Bedding is stacked everywhere, as if someone had tried to put everything away, quickly. It's difficult to overcome our curiosity so we open a few drawers – they're full of memories: postcards, letters, bills, old coins and notes, stocks, various objects as in any house, but all from a long time ago. But the most amazing finds are the photographs of life in Tokyo and of this family, which seems to have been extensive. One particularly striking picture shows the old man chatting with the British Queen! This completely changes the way we see this house and we decide to find out more about it and the two main characters, whose names seem to be John and Sugiko Jerwood.

In the other room is an expensive-looking painting of a much older woman, strict and severe looking. There's also a *butsudan* (a home altar to revere the dead) so this older woman was perhaps Sugiko's mother. She seems to have kept a pet pigeon, judging by all the pictures of him strutting around the house, and he even has his own little hut. He was called *Po-Po-Chan*. Cute?

We find another TV, the fourth. The photos in here show Hirohito and the Japanese royal family, surrounded by other photos of the family in this house. What are the links between all this? Another curious thing is a number of boxes wrapped in paper from the Okura Hotel, a renowned upmarket hotel in central Tokyo. By chance I come across John's address. He used to live in Tokyo. This address and the Okura Hotel could be an interesting start for my research.

Back in Tokyo. I first show up, a little innocently, at the Okura Hotel reception desk to check whether a certain Sugiko was still living here, knowing that to be almost impossible. *Oh! This was a long time ago!* I'm told, after five minutes of fierce battle with the old computer. *But these are private details.* Not knowing what to do next, I spend the afternoon exploring the hotel, talking to the old tenants of the stores and the café staff. Only two clerks remember the Jerwoods. According to them, the family was extremely wealthy and they could afford to live at the hotel. But as they didn't give me any clues or links to the old house I try the Tokyo address. Unfortunately there's absolutely nothing there, the site has been levelled.

So I go back to the abandoned house in the company of a Japanese friend, who soon finds a photo of a small temple with a *sotoba* (wooden board where Buddhists register a kind of prayer accompanied by the name of the deceased) clearly showing the family name. The temple in Tokyo was also mentioned – my next destination.

The family who own the temple live nearby. Trying my best to look like a foreign journalist, I knock at the door. Within seconds, an old man opens it. He knew the family, and although he doesn't remember very clearly he has some interesting details such as names, events and dates. I even get the chance to visit their tomb. John and Sugiko's names are on the same *sotoba* – there are no living relatives and they have no children. The tomb is rarely visited and maintained. Deeply moved, I say a little prayer for them. Their story is beginning to make sense.

In 1936, the young John had met Sugiko's brother Junji in Paris. He was a diplomat working for the Japanese government. Their encounter was somehow linked to the fact that John would take over his uncle's cultured pearl business and expand it to Japan. The family jewellery business based in London's Hatton Garden was already very successful. John must have met Sugiko around that time. In one of the photos I found, she was in London too. She was also extremely pretty. The business affair turned into a love affair. After serving in World War II, John moved to Tokyo.

The house was built in 1948 and he and Sugiko married in 1950. They did not however live in that house, it was for Sugiko's mother, Junji and sister Kiyomi, who all seem to have been showered with presents from John and Sugiko throughout their lives. The wealthy businessman set up the Jerwood Foundation in 1977 and became a generous benefactor in the fields of education and music – which explains the photo of him and Queen Elizabeth.

Eventually Sugiko moved to the Okura Hotel as John was often away on business. Kiyomi meanwhile was left alone at the Royal House when the other family members died, so she joined Sugiko to enjoy hotel life together. Ten more years passed. The Royal House grew dusty and almost forgotten. But I found proof that the family had visited – Kodak VR CP-100 negatives (available between 1983 and 1986) showing Kiyomi at the house.

John died of a heart attack in 1991 in New York. Sugiko stayed at the hotel until 1997 and died aged 78. Kiyomi stayed until 2004 and died at 91. The Okura Hotel then sent all their belongings in boxes back to the Royal House, where they were left at the entrance by the Yamato delivery service.

But this isn't the end. In this story redolent with old memories and ghosts, one person is still alive: a younger sister. She is called Kiyoko. At the temple I learned that she married and now belongs to another family. So the temple no longer has any link with Kiyoko, but I'm sure that, sometimes, she visits the old tomb of her former family.

I walk around the temple, hoping to find an old lady that might resemble her. The sun sets and home calls me.

I still hope to see her some day.

Schools

I've always liked abandoned Japanese schools. Not only are they sleeping beautifully far away, in forgotten parts of the countryside, but they're also the cradle of the Japanese soul. The way these little schools were run is still a reflection of Japanese society today and the education system, which is worth learning more about in order to understand the people.

Most of the abandoned schools I've visited in Japan are wooden constructions, not only because they're my favourites but they're also the most widespread. Most were built before or around World War II, but some are even from the Meiji period (1868–1912).

With the ageing population, the number of students dwindled over the years, from almost 12 million elementary-school students in 1980 to 6.8 million in 2012. There are now thousands of these little abandoned wooden schools scattered throughout the beautiful countryside.

Namezawa Elementary School
M小学校N分校
1873–1974

The route led me past Aokigahara forest, up a mountain road, then turned right up a narrow rocky path. I always rent basic cars and try my best to treat them gently. But sometimes the *haikyo* trips really demand a 4x4. I had to stop a few times on the way and shift fallen rocks to avoid damaging the car.

After a few kilometres along this forest path, I was beginning think I'd come to a dead end. Then a village came into view. A few houses, fields, everything wide open. At first I didn't see the school but eventually found it quietly surrounded by trees in a really pleasant site. There was only silence and all signs of life seemed so far away.

In front of the school is a statue of Ninomiya Sontoku, an eminent 19th-century philosopher and economist, who was born into a peasant family but studied on his own while working on the land. Then we entered the old shack, or maybe should I say time capsule.

Built in 1873, the wonderful smell of wood permeated everything. Old photos on the walls, the tables and chairs still lined up facing the blackboard. Everything was clean and tidy, ready for the students to get back to work. Only the spider webs and the thick layer of dust reminded us that there were no students in the playground.

Sakamoto Elementary School
坂本小学校
1868–1994

Okayama prefecture is a wonderland for *haikyo* explorers. Nobody would be surprised to meet a little boy there, followed by a talking dog, a monkey and a pheasant. His name is Momotaro and he's on a mission to defeat the *yokai* on the remote demon island of Onigashima.

Following ancient roads and going through forgotten villages, we finally arrived at Sakamoto's old school. We parked in the town and went up the hill where the school dozed quietly. The entrance was beautiful and the grass was still being looked after, evenly cut. The cicadas were happily singing and I realized that the backdrop was the mountains of Okayama, bathing in the warm sunlight at the end of the day.

The doors were all open and there was no difficulty at all accessing the site. The school was built back in 1868 but probably rebuilt and extended a few times until it was finally abandoned in 1994.

Urban explorers are very attracted to this school: it contains an old 3D anatomical model. This is another thing about urban exploration in Japan: most *haikyo* have their own specific and almost magical object, room or story. We all wish that nobody will take them away or alter them; that would be removing the heart of the *haikyo*.

Wooden School Den
K小学校
1920s–1970

As a great fan of Ghibli Studio animation movies and more specifically of their settings, I love the Japanese countryside, especially the little green hills with perhaps a few trees or rice fields dotted around. So I was more than delighted by this location.

Next to an old village was a hill covered by a verdant grove of trees, with stone steps leading up. It was like heading into the heart of some magical forest. We followed the steps and two minutes later the little school appeared.

With such a powerful ambiance, we could feel how life was really like here. The students going up those steps, in an orderly line. Everyone with the same type of schoolbag, passed down within the family. During their first day at school, they learned how to arrange their books and pencils on the desk, stand up and sit down at the right time, take notes and ask questions. Lunches were eaten in those little classrooms; the students all had a different *bento* (lunch box) prepared by their families, which they willingly shared with each other.

These little countryside schools were like a second home and family for the students.

North Korean schools
1970s–1998

This is as paradoxical as it gets but Japan has many North Korean schools. The Japanese occupied Korea for forty years before World War II and during this time many Koreans migrated to Japan. After the Japanese defeat, those Koreans regained their nationality with the right to stay on Japanese territory. In 1965, the Japanese recognized South Korea as a legitimate government and the Koreans in Japan were allowed to choose the new South Korean nationality. Those who didn't do so automatically became North Koreans, usually proud of their origins and having many differences with the new, Americanized, South Korea. They decided to build their own schools through the ethnic activist and de facto North Korean embassy, the Chongryon association, financed by the Pyongyang government. There are still about 10,000 students in Japan's North Korean schools.

I've visited two of these, both abandoned in 1998. Except for a few books and products shipped from Pyongyang, they've been badly vandalized. Nobody looks after them any more and it seems that people would rather have them demolished were it not for the huge cost. The lack of love for those *haikyo* is palpitant.

In Tokyo, there are active Korean schools and even the Korea University, which is often accused of spreading North Korean ideology. Student numbers are falling every year due to the identity issues they have to face.

Kajika Elementary School

This little coastal town is lovely. The cute harbour looks exactly like the one depicted in the *Ponyo* movie about the goldfish who befriends a five-year-old boy. The school was in the town centre and we had to climb a flight of steps to reach it.

The playground was exceptionally clean. I looked around for a while then decided to wait for my friends outside, as it was a lucky day of beautiful weather in the middle of June. As I was patiently sitting outside, half-asleep, an old man walked up the steps and I worried that he might be annoyed about our break-in. Not at all: he was glad to find us there. He'd been a student at this school sixty years ago, and since it closed thirty years ago he'd come by every day and cleaned up the grounds. He lived nearby so this task was a pleasure for him. In Japan the students themselves usually clean their schools, and the fact that this old man took his job so seriously was a joy to see.

As we headed back to our car his wife called out to us. *I made dinner, please join us!* We refused nicely and left the overwhelmingly friendly little town. On the way, I couldn't help but think that those two warm-hearted people must have met in that school, a long, long time ago. They're still together today. This old man is keeping their meeting place sweet and clean. I looked back and even though I hadn't spent much time there, I felt a rush of melancholy in having visited somebody else's little paradise.

Hospitals

Talking about urban exploration and abandoned hospitals, what tends to come to mind are modern buildings with long corridors, wards full of beds and sets of surgical lamps. Their exteriors aren't particularly exciting and most of the rooms have been cleared of all their equipment. But in Japan, abandoned hospitals have a very unique and local identity.

The hospitals attract me most among all *haikyo*, especially the early wooden ones. I feel as if they possess magical powers, so as you walk around mysterious encounters tend to happen. Rather like dilapidated wooden houses with an old doll at the entrance, a rotting chair, weird instruments, enchanted-looking potions, an old surgical bed and few teeth are all that's left. That's the spirit. It's an awakening dream or a nightmare to visit these places.

Clinic of the Little Brain
S医院
1910s–1970s

The Clinic of the Little Brain was in a secluded place next to a rice distributor. That was the first surprise of the day for me: I didn't even know those kinds of distributors still existed. The little clinic, seen from the outside, was quite gloomy. At first it looked like an abandoned wooden house with its old rusty portal. That's how most clinics looked that were built in Japan during the Meiji and Taishō periods. This one dated from the end of World War I.

We went in tentatively, as the owner still lived next door and we could easily be seen and heard. The first room was a waiting room and pharmacy. Behind was the room where the medicine was kept, still some lying about. On the left was the examination room. We could imagine the doctor in here, his desk overflowing with documents, pictures on the wall and comfortable chairs. There was also a little couch like the kind therapists use. This clinic probably dealt with both physical and mental health problems.

The room behind it was far more chilling. On the dirty floor stood an old operating table and a sink for the doctor to wash his hands and implements. We grew uncomfortable, especially when we found a jar containing a tiny little brain. It was very common at that time to preserve the organs of dead patients in order to analyse them later.

Sergeant Clinic
S医院
1914–1996

I had the oddest feeling when we arrived in front of the Sergeant Clinic in Nagoya, in a very residential area. The place had a special aura but also some kind of unsettled atmosphere – it just didn't feel right.

When the clinic was built in 1914, it was probably a smaller wooden construction. Later, a new and ugly concrete façade was added, changing its appearance. Passers-by were trying to avoid looking at the ghostly structure. The local residents stayed away from this place and their feeling is understandable.

The clinic was plunged in dark and had obviously been vandalized. It looked like a murder scene. I went up the fragile stairs, cautiously. There, carefully labelled, I found hundreds of tiny bottles containing organs, all looking very similar. All that was written on the labels was "formalin" (ホルマリン), giving no clues as to what the samples were. Also mentioned on the bottle was the gender of the person. It was surprising to find those mesmerizing and strange objects untouched after all this time – the clinic closed in 1996.

After this gruesome discovery, I took some time to relax downstairs, looking at the old photos and belongings those people had left. They seem to have been a happy family after all.

The Doctor's Shack

S診療所
1930s–1970s

In the countryside, north of Nagoya, you might come across a little shack hidden at the back of a beautiful shrine. The Doctor's Shack is a very quiet old wooden clinic, in lovely surroundings with an enchanting stream running by. A dream place for a lovely day in the sun, feet in the water, and the cicadas – *semi* in Japanese – singing in the background.

Entering the house I had the feeling it was almost untouched, everything was so ancient. As if I was the first person to visit in the past fifty years. But this is one of the best-known abandoned clinics in Japan. It features in *Nippon no Haikyo*, a book referencing 200 *haikyo* throughout Japan, together with maps.

There was truly something mystical about the place. Maybe it was the dilapidated wooden structure, or all the medical objects from a long-gone era, or maybe it was because it was hidden in an idyllic jungle full of mysteries … and mosquitoes! The creaking of the wood from time to time gave the impression that the old forgotten shack was still alive.

The best-loved part of the shack can be seen from reception, through a small window where the pharmacist would pass the drugs over to his customers: an old apothecary, an old-time pharmacist, reminding me of the pre-war period depicted in Ghibli movies.

We could imagine a doctor with round glasses walking around, unsmiling. He loved taking out patients' organs for analysis. Then, in the evening, illuminated by the moon and a small oil lamp on his desk, he would make up his own medicines. His prescriptions weren't always intended to cure the patient straight away, but rather to experiment and observe the effect.

This image might seem harsh but it might even be kinder than the actual truth. During World War II, Japanese doctors were known to use patients, especially prisoners, as guinea pigs. Sometimes cutting out their organs or immersing them in boiling water to see how long they could survive. The infamous Unit 731 that the Japanese operated in China was known for such atrocities, but at the time such experiments were conducted in Japan too.

The only inmates of this clinic during my visit were a tribe of bloodthirsty mosquitoes. Surely the spirit of the doctor lived on in them.

Ghost's Clinic
F医院
1930s–1962

Clearly I'm addicted to Japan's abandoned clinics. I've visited many of them, looking for something particularly odd and mysterious that would send me to an alternative place between the past and my imagination. I loved most of them but something was always lacking, the atmosphere was never truly *complete*. Until the day I travelled to the island of Shikoku.

It was a long drive to the Ghost's Clinic in Tokushima prefecture. As I'd never seen any pictures of the interior, this was a gamble. I'd no idea if the place was worth seeing or even if it was still there. This is part of the *haikyo* game. The only photo I'd ever seen was a glimpse through a slightly open window. A colourful shot in the dark.

The first thrill came when we finally came across the beautiful place itself. *It's there! And it's abandoned!* Three big wooden houses surrounded by trees, swamped in green foliage. Next door, an old woman was working in her vegetable garden, ignoring our presence completely.

I pushed open the squeaky door, wondering what I was about to discover.

Once inside we found ourselves in a small waiting room with a single chair. It was completely dark. The floor and the structure in general were in a very bad state so we stepped carefully. We could see a passage leading to the examination room. On the right, the pharmacy counter, where drugs and payments were exchanged through a little opening in the wall. Behind it, colours glittering in the darkness.

It was filled with stars! All of them shining. It was an old apothecary, the most impressive I'd ever seen. This was exactly what the photo I'd found depicted. I took a close look, trying to read the labels. One of them was Coramine, a stimulant used against tranquilizer overdoses, now banned. I've only seen it in the Philippines, to feed the fighting cocks. I stayed in the apothecary over an hour, looking at everything from every angle.

There were two examination rooms. One of them had an old comfy-looking dentist chair with a wooden desk in front. The scene was beautiful even though it lacked light. The second room looked more like a study with books in German and even more magical potions.

The rest of the house consisted of dining room and bedrooms, all empty. I tried to find the most recent of a pile of old newspapers, which seemed to be 1962. I really wonder how the locals feel about living all their life next to this place.

The Mental Asylum
A病院
1940s–2001

I gathered with my fellow explorers in a relatively new residential area near Tokyo around lunchtime. The fence ran alongside the houses and at first it seemed that there was no easy way in but luckily we found a small gap. We jumped through carefully to avoid being seen by people living nearby. Inside was another metal fence, again with a gap in it.

This, my first visit to a psychiatric hospital, was a truly great experience. After a few steps I fell in love with the spookiness of the place. This *haikyo* had a unique atmosphere, totally different from the old wooden clinics I'm used to. It almost felt as if it was from Western urbex ruins. The basement, a long corridor studded with barred windows on both sides like a prison, was by far the most interesting section. The cells were very small, with only Turkish toilets and sometimes a wheelchair in the corner. There were stains that looked like blood on the walls. My friend whispered that this hospital was known for patients committing suicide by throwing themselves against the walls …

The eeriest fact about the abandoned asylum was its extreme sensitivity to the wind. There were slamming doors, dancing blinds and cracking ceilings. We felt ourselves to be in the belly of a beast in agony, full of ghosts and monsters, and stayed close together during the whole experience.

Clinic Z
Z医院
1910s–1980s

The mysterious Clinic Z was discovered by a *haikyo* explorer in the '90s and then completely forgotten. Our hobby was not such a big thing at that time, mostly only locals exploring the ruins of their neighbourhood. In the 2000s, *haikyo* became increasingly popular and even more so through social media networks.

Clinic Z is, as far as I know, the oldest abandoned clinic in Japan. It was a real delight to the eye, especially with the sinking golden sun and the white snow: it looked ancient, smelled ancient, felt ancient, the machines and tools inside were so old it seemed they could turn to dust at a touch. Inside, there was of course the doctor's room but also an operating theatre, a scanner room, and many private rooms in which the doctor and his family would spend their spare time.

What struck me most was the doctor's examination room. It was all in beautiful wood and the soft colours were quite unreal. A perfect set for a movie. The operating theatre was state of the art: at the time, there was no special lighting for operations and so they'd installed a glass window in the roof to provide even light of high quality.

The Zed Clinic deserves to be a museum but the owner is apparently planning to demolish it completely.

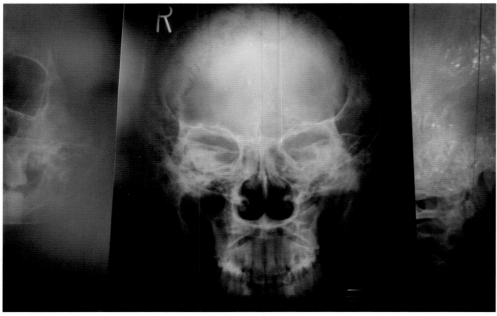

Tuberculosis Sanatorium
貝塚の結核療養所
1943–1992

Sadly it wasn't a beautiful day when we arrived and the tuberculosis sanatorium itself was rather a sorry sight. It was hard to imagine that a few decades ago kids had been playing around this huge tasteless block of concrete. The building, which closed in 1992, has been repeatedly vandalized since then.

The Tuberculosis Sanatorium for Children was built in 1943 as the government tried to manage the treatment for this highly contagious disease. With some success apparently, as it closed due to lack of patients.

There were still some machines and equipment in the hospital. The X-ray machines and MRI scanners had made the place famous in the *haikyo* community as some of the images depict organs, sometimes even babies. But you might wonder how such a hospital could have been abandoned while leaving all this personal information behind.

I'd like to believe that most of the kids survived tuberculosis thanks to this hospital, though a Japanese friend told me she could sense their ghosts in this place. For her, it was the most haunted abandoned hospital she'd ever visited in Japan.

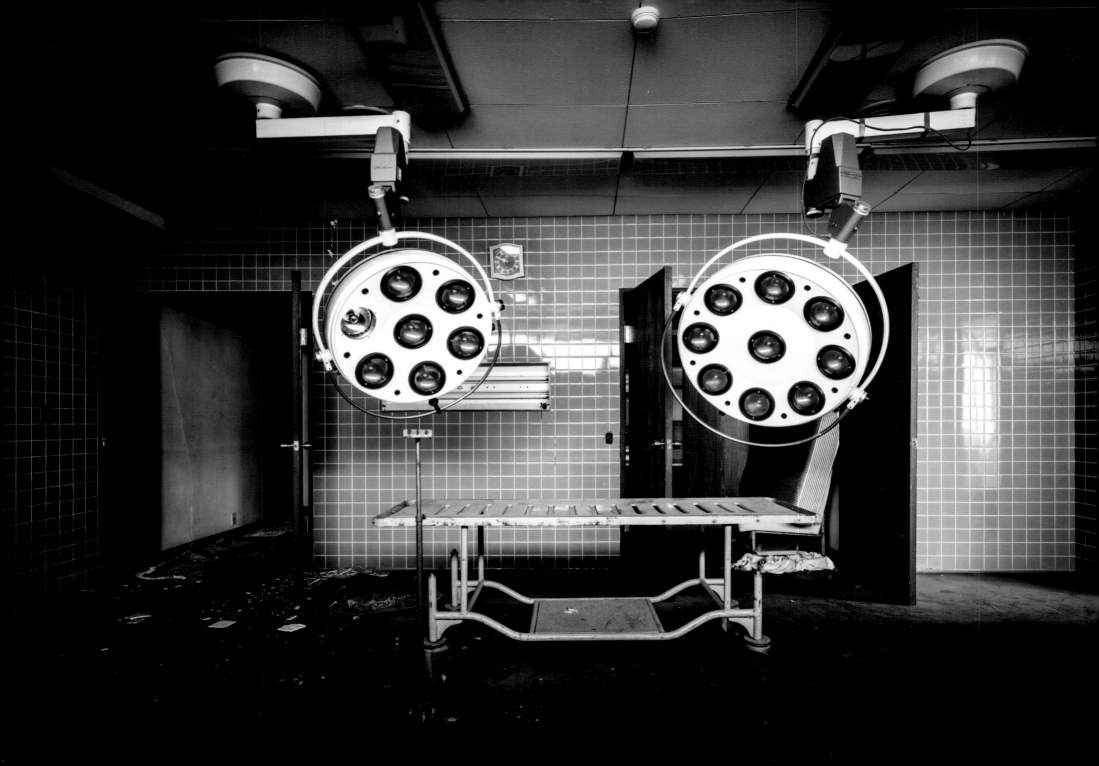

Surgical Lights Necropolis
勿忘草色の手術室

In the middle of the most boring and dying town in Japan there stands a dreadful clinic. We named it simply the *Surgical Lights Necropolis*.

We discovered that the owner seems to have enjoyed a pretty good life. He was probably the richest guy in town and owned a huge property nearby with a magnificent modern house.

This clinic must have been a very prosperous business for a few decades before being abandoned in 1998, but it's now totally run down and impossible to rehabilitate.

The clinic was really gloomy and smelled terrible but was filled with artefacts, the best among them definitely the surgical lights in the operating theatre. What a surprise – I never thought I'd get the chance to see such a set of lights in a Japanese ruin.

Smallpox Isolation Ward
東伊豆町隔離病舎
1958–1982

Izu peninsula, one of my favourite regions of Japan, was the site of the Smallpox Isolation Ward. In an atmosphere similar to that of the TV series *Lost*, we passed between two mountains in a lush forest next to the ocean to visit this crumbling old *haikyo*. The birds were singing, we could hear the distant sound of the sea echoing on the mountains and feel the freshness of nature. The sight of this very odd, long wooden building in the middle of nowhere somehow felt completely expected.

It was exciting to explore the bowels of this wooden beast and discover each and every room. There were only straw beds, wobbly windows, sinks and some small trinkets. Unlike other hospitals, there was nothing hidden or shocking about this place.

But wasn't it haunted by the dead people's spirits? My friend who can see ghosts thought it was, but that they're all happy; they already knew they would have to leave the world of the living. They were kindly treated at the sanatorium, they had a peaceful end and they can still roam this beautiful place.

We walked back through the fresh leaves. A beautiful day in a small corner of paradise with a melancholic *haikyo*. With the thoughts that people must have died happily here, we left with a smile.

Leisure and pleasure

My passion for *haikyo* started a few years after I moved to Tokyo. Thanks to a work colleague I discovered an excellent Japanese website called Haikyo Deflation Spiral. He shared with me an incredible picture taken from it: a huge abandoned ferris wheel hidden in the middle of a forest. My passion for *haikyo* did not unfold right away, but the picture of this abandoned big wheel remained engraved in my memory for years. Neither was I particularly attracted to photography, as everybody was taking pictures, everywhere, all the time. It didn't strike me as the thing to do. At that time I was just using a small camera to record memories only. Then photographer friends persuaded me to buy my first DSLR and I never looked back.

I needed a shooting subject for the weekend and this image of the ferris wheel came to mind. I discovered it had been demolished some time ago but, still excited about the idea of taking photographs of something abandoned, I checked out the new keyword I'd learned: *haikyo*. The second website I discovered was Michael John Grist's, where he mentioned the *Nippon no Haikyo* book, which I bought right away and read his article about the exploration of the abandoned water park, Izu Sports World. At the age of 18 I had jumped a fence to explore a water park in my hometown. Called Aqualand, it was closed during the winter – not abandoned although it looked that way. I still had vibrant memories of this exploration so Izu Sports World would take me back in time. I went there with a friend who taught me photography on the spot, and I knew immediately that a passion was born. Theme parks also became my first-love *haikyo* and I wanted to see more of them.

An enormous number of *haikyo* are related to leisure – they are the dust generated by the explosion of the financial bubble.

In the '80s, Japan vigorously boosted its economy: loans were made easier, there was plenty of cash around and Japanese salaries were from 30 to 40 per cent higher than those of Europeans. People bought and speculated by every means. New factories, apartment buildings, hotels, golf courses, resorts and theme parks were built and the champagne flowed. But the speculative bubble finally exploded on 29 December 1989. Two years later, the value of the Nikkei stock market index plummeted more than 50 per cent and has never really stopped falling since.

A land of abandoned strange-looking shops, humongous hotels, sex empires and theme parks about anything and everything was born as a side effect. To some people's delight.

Maya Hotel
摩耶観光ホテル
1929–1994

Maya Hotel, aka Mayakan, is a celebrity among *haikyo* in Japan. So many people have been there, done all sorts of things, taken all the photos you could imagine. For those who like *haikyo*, the Maya Hotel is a must-see. I went there twice, once using the Maya Ropeway which leads lazy explorers straight to the place, and the second time via a forbidden hiking path. The second option is more interesting and makes the experience magical and enjoyable.

The hotel was opened originally as social benefit for Maya Ropeway, four years after the company set up their business. There is a road to the top of Mount Maya and buses run up there, but they all end at Hoshi station, the last stop on the ropeway. Maya Hotel is actually halfway along the ropeway, and only the dangerous hiking path leads to its door.

Although the hotel was opened a long time ago, it has been closed for long periods. During its years of existence it suffered major damage from the air raids of World War II, the Great Hanshin earthquake of 1995 and various other disasters like typhoons. It was shut down, sold and refurbished a number of times, but nothing worked out well. It has even been known as a *haikyo* once before, when it was abandoned for fifteen years after the war.

We all know about the tyre from a heavy bomber that has somehow found its way onto the balcony of Mayakan. If you check photos taken around 2002, you'll find that this tyre was once stuck in the roof. There's a popular belief that it was dropped during wartime air raids and then used as some kind of decoration, even featuring in a video clip by a band called *Action*.

The symbolic part of the Maya Hotel is the Green Room, the destination for all visiting photographers. The floor is completely disintegrating and seems to have fallen in. Apparently, before the war, the Green Room was a bathroom with old-fashioned tiled bathtubs. These went out of use and a new floor was laid over the bathtubs. Now the wood is rotten with gaping holes everywhere. But the best thing about this room is its extraordinary lighting. The windows always seem to glow with the greenness of the natural world outside, even in winter.

I've been told that the ghosts of the waiters are still working the room while a few customers are dancing. That must be a beautiful sight.

Massive hotels

Japan built a plethora of massive hotels that all went bankrupt. The beautiful Izu peninsula, once known as the Hawaii of Japan, became famous for its huge abandoned hotels. Tourists are always taken aback on their first visit to Atami, a city that was once a resort. But driving along the coastline is still a wonderful experience and the *haikyoist* can always find an abandoned hotel or *ryokan* (Japanese traditional inn) to visit.

As these aren't usually kept secret like other types of *haikyo*, information on them is easy to find. If life takes you to Izu peninsula one day, you can check out a few such as the Okawa Grand Hotel, Okawa Seminar House, Shimoda View Hotel or Dialand Hotel.

Abandoned hotels can be found everywhere. There are so many of them that they've even become boring for local explorers. Personally, I loved visiting the Rainbow Hotel in Okayama for its surprising graffiti, observation tower and very graphic escalator. Then there is the Sunpark Hotel in Yamanashi, really gloomy with its rooms thick with asbestos and its old-fashioned restaurant. Finally, the Nakagusuku Kogen Hotel in Okinawa, a gigantic concrete monster with splendid views over the exotic island.

The *Haikyo* Cow
廃牛

This is an abandoned cow shed, but not only that. It's also the cutest *haikyo* that became famous for unique quirkiness and an agreeable stopover for explorers passing through.

It was once used as a little shop selling delicious milky ice cream. But some say it might have been part of a theme park or even a karaoke venue.

Haikyo explorers have even launched a special day of celebration, known as the *Haikyo* Cow Day.

廃牛の日

It is held on 19 August.

Love hotels

Love hotels, despite their kitsch looks, are relatively new in Japan. They popped up for the first time in Osaka in 1968 and they're used by different kinds of people. Young lovers usually meet there secretly, entering by different doors. They'll rent a room for two or three hours and then leave the love hotel, again on separate paths, and go home. The truth is that their best clients are drunken salarymen. For these corporate employees, wandering the streets far from home, it's easy to go where a light is shining and there's no doubt that love hotels draw the eye. I recommend visiting the streets of Shibuya and Ikebukuro, where the ambiance is quite special.

There are about 40,000 love hotels in Japan. As this is an easy business to run the hotels are built as fast as possible and abandoned if they fail – it'll work somewhere else! Older love hotels can't keep up with the new ones though, especially out in the remote countryside, so they're simply closed up and forgotten by the owners.

Haikyo love hotels are, for the most part, not very attractive. But they can be very gloomy and their unsettling decoration can make for an epic day's exploration. In the little hills of Chiba, I especially enjoyed discovering two love hotels. The Fuurin Hotel has country-themed rooms and the Yui Grand Love Hotel has supposed bloodstains on the walls and a weird story about a serial killer. Not sure if all the stories I've heard about happenings in *haikyo* are true, but they're sure cheaper and scarier than any ghost houses you'll find in theme parks!

House of Hidden Treasures
道祖神の里
1978–1997

When you've seen all the famous *onsen* (hot baths) in Japan, you always want to see more. I'm addicted to them and always willing to venture off the beaten path to visit older examples. They're often a promised land for *haikyo* and adult leisure.

The House of Hidden Treasures is a sex museum near an *onsen* village in Yamaguchi prefecture in the south. I had high expectations of this museum as the Japanese adult entertainment world has become so well known for its sexual eccentricities and strange fantasies.

The museum, closed since 1997, looked like a Japanese house or restaurant from outside but seemed out of place. The inside was completely different, more like caves interconnected by tunnels.

Cloaked in darkness, the museum was really gloomy, although its content was pleasanter that anything I'd imagined. There were funny, happy phallic rocks looking at you everywhere, huge dickheads guarding the tunnels, a sex shrine for everlasting love-making happiness. But the last room had human dolls and dildos laid out in glass coffins. I'm not sure what happened when you pressed the buttons but I can imagine.

Akeno Gekijo Strip Club
明野劇場
1970–1994

Akeno Gekijo is a strip club of the '70s in the funereal back yard of a series of unexciting love hotels, located in such a boring part of Ibaraki prefecture it makes you wonder how they ever attracted enough customers.

At the end of the '80s, adult videos became really popular in Japan and entertainment outside the big cities took a big hit, many going out of business. I've no idea what happened to the Akeno Gekijo but it had to close in 1994. A year later it was set on fire and this new carbonized version became notorious for its unique appearance.

My visit was pretty surprising. The main stage was still there, stretching out from the far end to occupy most of the room; seating like in old cinemas; ten big stage lights that must have created a bewitching sort of ambiance. There were stage-like elevated walkways as well. On the second floor was a projection room that was a delight, like being aboard some kind of anachronistic spaceship.

Izari Health Center
お水荘ヘルスピア
1989–2007

My first visit to the island of Shikoku was great fun as there are so many *haikyo* there and the roads are beautiful, whether alongside the infinite-looking Pacific Ocean or up in the hills and mountains. We were also blessed by stormy but enjoyable weather which varied the play of light wonderfully.

The only way of reaching the Izari Health Center was by a tiringly long and narrow winding road. The huge complex included a hotel with many rooms, restaurant, gym and, of course, the aquatic park itself with sliding tubes and swimming pools. There was also a beautiful view of the ocean which certainly was a big plus in the success of this place.

Unfortunately, it seems not to have been financially viable and was abandoned in 2007. Tokushima prefecture not being particularly well-known for its youthfulness might be one of the reasons the place closed down.

Gluck Kingdom
グリュック王国
1989–2007

We were in beautiful Hokkaido for a weekend break, not blessed at all by the weather. I used the constant drizzly rain as a good excuse to explore the many places in the Obihiro area where we could eat *butadon*, a sensationally delicious pork dish. You must try it.

Arriving at the entrance of Gluck Kingdom, an abandoned theme park, we were met with a low barbed-wire fence with the corpse of a life-size doll attached to it, together with *Keep Out* and *No Entry* signs.

This *haikyo* didn't seem very friendly. I was also concerned about the local residents, more specifically the bears, which had been spotted strolling in the park by other explorers. The local police were also very active, constantly checking if anyone was trespassing so they could hand out an expensive entry ticket. But as we'd come so far, at this point we couldn't really afford to hesitate. We parked the car out of sight and jumped over the fence.

After a hundred metres, a huge parking lot opened up before us. The sky cleared, the rain stopped, and it seemed we were in luck after all. The only thing missing was a few bear cubs to come and play with us, but without their mother.

We unhesitatingly entered a windmill and found ourselves inside a medieval German castle. The park had been very well built – they even imported the paving from Germany for greater authenticity. Behind the castle there's also a vast theme park with roller coasters and a ferris wheel. If the weather had been better I'd have spent the whole day making the most of the photo opportunities.

My Japanese teacher had been to the park in the '90s and she showed me a few photos taken at the time: it was already a ghost town. She added that many of the shops were stocked with Japanese rather than German products.

The lack of visitors inevitably led the park to close its huge doors sometime in 2007 – a sad day for Hokkaido prefecture as it was part of a marketing plan to attract visitors to various parts of the island, all with their own theme park.

So how about some more *butadon*?

Russian Village
ロシア村
1993–2002

The Russian Village is one of the first abandoned leisure parks in Japan that I'd seen pictures of. Paradoxically, it's also the one I visited last. Being very popular, I knew it had been heavily vandalized: the hotels were set on fire and all the windows smashed. I love the fact that *haikyo* are relatively pristine ruins but this place seemed to be an exception.

It was built in 1993 in Niigata prefecture and a number of Russians were hired to make it more authentic. In the park they built a gigantic hotel, a replica of Suzdal Church, shops and a circus.

My fellow explorer on this occasion is probably the youngest I know. Not afraid of much, except bears, Mimi-chan braves all kinds of *haikyo* and takes beautiful photos. I love travelling with people who see things differently, it's like discovering a place with a new mindset.

The park was a wreck, as I'd thought, but we had an aim: to find the stuffed mammoth. The sun was not that high in the sky any more and the shadows were fast lengthening. The mammoth was nowhere to be seen but finally, at the far end of the park, we found it. This is one photograph we had to come home with.

Yamaguchi New Zealand Farm
1990–2005

This New Zealand Farm is only suitable for perfect weather, with a pleasant breeze and a relaxed heart. This is one of the very few *haikyo* where you don't feel like a trespasser; no worries about guards or police, plenty of open space and fresh air, nothing really dangerous or disturbing, and the only sounds you hear are frogs croaking and birds singing. Just as you would imagine New Zealand.

The founder, a farmer's son, opened the first Farm Park on his father's land. The concept of Farm Parks has a profound meaning in Japan, an attempt to make good use of farmland going to waste because of the dwindling population in the countryside. Such parks also create employment opportunities and the chance for people to sell farm products inside and around the park. Unfortunately, three out of four New Zealand Parks are out of business already, and this one closed in 2005.

The weather was unsettled all day, but as dusk began to fall the skies gained some amazing shades of pink. Smelling the freshness after the rain, we walked faster to capture the fascinating change of light. It was as if we were already in heaven.

A light breeze carried the summer heat away and hidden birds sang melodies we'd never heard before.

Tenkaen: China Park of Heaven
天華園
1992–1997

The Tenkaen pagoda could be clearly seen from a distance among the foliage. We parked not far from the entrance. Nobody was around and the park was only enclosed by a very low barrier, so we expected a very enjoyable and easy exploration.

The atmosphere was so realistic it reminded me of my year in China, where I was a student but spent most of my time backpacking around the country. This park had the same fragrances as a few old towns I'd visited in Yunnan: shades of ochre, worm-eaten wood.

The state of decay added some positive character to the place and we could imagine ourselves in Beijing's Summer Palace had it been left to the ravages of time. Everything was there, the Moon Gate, the pagoda and a rock-filled garden. Kunming Stone Forest? I ended up at the top of the pagoda for a global view of the glorious flowers, another highlight of this park.

Tenkaen, like Gluck Kingdom, was part of the marketing plan to attract visitors to Hokkaido. At least it worked for a few local *haikyoists* and foreign urban explorers.

The park, built in 1992, closed only five years later.

Kejonuma Leisure Land
化女沼レジャーランド
1979–2000

Kejonuma Leisure Land is an amusement park built in 1979, just another victim of the financial bubble. Driving through Tohoku on the road leading to the park, the cracked concrete that seemed beyond repair made me wonder if the park was not completely crumbling too. But luckily, and just a few months after the Tohoku earthquake in 2011, the little ferris wheel was still standing.

The site at the "Pond of the Ghost Woman" (literal translation of Kejonuma) had a faded loveliness. There were still a few attractions visible: a merry-go-round, kart racing, coffee stalls and some adventure attractions, and it even had its own little golf course.

The ferris wheel is the most obvious attraction: old, rusty, but still proudly upright. I strolled around for over an hour, admiring it from every angle. This vibrant *bhavacakra* (Buddhist wheel of life) became one of my favourite *haikyo*. I'd had this image in my mind for such a long time and here it was, finally in front of me.

The park closed in 2000 but was never officially abandoned by the owner.

Western Village
ウエスタン村
1973–2007

Once known as the Kinugawa Ranch, this village was built around 1973. At the time it was a very simple place where visitors could enjoy cowboy-style activities. The owner, a local man called Ominami-san, said that "the purpose in life is not to earn money but to make dreams come true" and that is basically what he did. The ranch became a proper theme park in 1975 and was renamed Western Village.

This *haikyo*, near Nikko in Tochigi prefecture, is easily accessible on a one-day trip from Tokyo, so I had plenty of chances to visit.

The entrance is practically unprotected and has many openings that make access easy for anyone. The owner perhaps stopped caring about trying to keep the new breed of tourists out. A stream divides Western Village into two – the actual village, extremely Far West ambiance with barber, bank, prison, saloons … everything is here, just like a movie set – and the "Mexican" side.

Crossing the stream by a cranky old bridge, I realized that it represented the Rio Grande. Rather unsettlingly, there was a range of laser guns on the riverbank aimed at targets on the Mexican side. This was wilder and interesting in its own way, with palm trees and dense vegetation, houses and barns in the middle. I followed a rail track and came across two old steam locomotives in the rear of the park.

Ominami-san extended his theme park each year, to the detriment of his profit margin. In 1995, he even added a replica of the famous Mount Rushmore, seemingly on an impulse.

The park closed in 2007 and is now virtually forgotten. But from time to time, tourists driving around the Nikko area are taken aback by this Japanese version of Mount Rushmore that looms up for a second and they have to come back to check it isn't a hallucination!

Nara Dreamland
The Abandoned Disneyland

奈良ドリームランド
1961–2006

The last spirits are leaving this abandoned theme park on the outskirts of Nara. It closed in 2006, after the number of visitors dropped dramatically in the aftermath of the opening of the new Tokyo Disneyland and Osaka Universal Studio.

Nara Dreamland used to be quite famous. It was built in 1961, six years after the original Disneyland in California. The layout is entirely based on Disneyland and negotiations took place with Walt Disney himself. Despite all that it failed. Importing a Western concept to Japan is usually difficult with endless red tape, and the American company was unwilling to have its brand adulterated. But the end result is good for *haikyoists*: here we have an abandoned Disneyland, ideal for a romantic walk by day or by night.

Knowing the official entrance to be completely blocked, I had to find another way to slip in.

The night before, driving slowly around the abandoned park looking for a possible entrance, a loud monotonous voice from a speaker scared me half to death. I couldn't understand exactly what it was about but later learned that it was a request not to dump garbage!

It's early morning and we're walking around the Nara Dreamland parking lot, still looking for an entrance. But wait, we aren't alone here. A guy with a big dog is approaching. Could he be a guard? Then we realize he's only a local taking a peaceful stroll with his dog.

He assures us there'd be no problem so we carry on and eventually find a way in round the back of the lot.

It's a wonderful summer day to visit the park. We walk by a huge wooden roller coaster and approach the main entrance, very welcoming with Nara Dreamland spelled out on the gateway.

All the shops and restaurants are empty, but the tables and chairs are still inside. One of them, My Neighbor Totoro, seems to have been a Ghibli outlet. As they couldn't sell any Disney products I guess they had to try and sell the local ones.

There's supposed to be some kind of security system here, and I've often heard of people getting caught. We walk carefully on, paying attention to every sound, but it's hard to relax because there's all sorts of activity going on just outside.

There's no Mickey or Minnie around but Nara Dreamland has its own set of characters, two of them omnipresent: Ran-chan and Dori-chan.

The wagons of the Screw Coaster must be fused to its rails, they're so rusted. Would it still be possible to rehabilitate this obsolete park and restart the whole business, or has it no future? Its only source of income seems to be catching all the unlucky curious trespassers and fining them 100,000 yen each. Maybe that covers the guards' salaries and the land taxes?

I walk on the burning hot rails and the summer heat rushes to my head. First-class sensation: walking on the rusty rails of an abandoned roller coaster, still slippery with the morning dew, under a magnificent blue sky and the singing of the frogs (and the Japanese cicadas) is a real treat.

The huge wooden Aska roller coaster is condemned, although it's not that old (built in 1998) and the company has tried in vain to sell it. It's now far too decrepit to survive dismantling and reassembling somewhere else. The vegetation is thick here. But what an impressive ride – just over a kilometre. It's going to be difficult to walk the length of it, so I just try to reach its highest point at 30 m. A few planks give way, making the climb more dangerous than expected. Good shoes and no fear of heights obligatory.

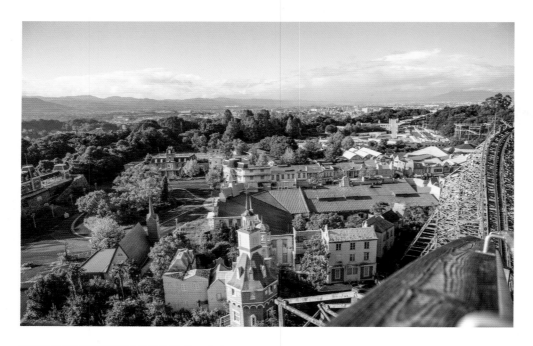

Walking below the vast ascent of Aska, I wonder at the huge complexity of the roller-coaster structure, a real maze of wooden planks, a kind of castle, very supple and with a smell of decayed resin. From the top there's a great view over Dreamland, but it's also one of the most dangerous spots. The planks are cracking under my weight and I have to walk on the central rail where the train used to run.

After a few minutes I'm looking down at the park entrance to the left, Main Street USA leading to Cinderella's Castle in the centre, and behind that the water park. You can even see the city of Nara, surrounded by mountains. Magic! The best thing about these wooden roller coasters is that they shake when you walk on them — not very reassuring — and it sure gives you the shivers.

Nara Dreamland has plenty of charm during the day but it's always difficult to take interesting shots in bright sunlight. But by night the park turns into an enchanted place.

Better to appreciate it silently.

Industrial

The industrialization of Japan started with the Meiji restoration in 1868 and reached near vertical growth during and after World War II. Sadly, wars are an economy booster for the countries involved. Japan's mining industries and productivity were at their peak during the Korean War, provisioning the UN allied forces. Because of the strictness of the Japanese Army, the new young workforce flowing into the economy after the war was extremely disciplined and willing to work very hard. Today's most powerful Japanese companies have grown from these roots.

There are four kinds of countries in the world: developed countries,
undeveloped countries, Japan and Argentina.
Simon Kuznets

This quote from the 1971 Nobel Prizewinner for Economics is no longer true and the Japanese economy has been going downhill since the '90s. Its exceptional workforce has been slowly disappearing, the population ageing and the will to be best evaporating. The mining industry declined as competition grew from South-East Asia, and the buildings were just left to rot as there was no question of using the limited funds of local government to clear all those sites. So welcome to the land of *kawaii* (cute) and the *sōshokukei danshi* (herbivore guys – kind of asexual and anti-corporate "grasseaters") – previous generations could never have imagined the situation today. None of the *haikyo* presented in this section are at all representative of modern Japan.

I have to admit that my heart probably lies in the Japan of the '60s when the steampunk industries were still powerful, surrounded by local farmers harvesting rice. I like to think life was hard but rewarding during those days, and that's the land I dream of exploring.

Mimi-chan arouses me from my thoughts. *A bear! That's a bear!* This is the first time she's seen a bear, and my second, but it's still an unbelievable sight. Those big empty spaces that once reverberated with constant noise are now a wonderland for wildlife. But be extremely careful visiting industrial sites – they're the most dangerous type of *haikyo* but also the most adventurous and exciting.

Shiraishi Mine
白石鉱山
1921–1969

Back in 1969, a typhoon hit Mie prefecture. The limestone mine of Shiraishi couldn't withstand the stresses. Its gigantic wooden shelves collapsed and most of the white powder stored there was washed away by the rain – the last straw for the mine, which closed down its operations.

A calcium carbonate product called *hakuenka* (白艷華), which was first made in the factory here, is exported throughout the world even today by the same company, Shiraishi, which owns other still-active mines. This factory is cleverly designed so a shame it's been abandoned. Looking down the mountainside, you can see that it's built along the slope with the river at its foot, so the entire complex can be supplied with electricity generated solely by the power of water from the peaks.

The day we visited was beautiful, without a cloud in the sky. Perfect for a hike through the green foliage enveloping Shiraishi Mine. We leapt through the rubble, feeling like Alice in a perfect Wonderland. The icy spring next to the parking lot offered a fine end to the day. At first we thought it might be river water and perhaps polluted. But on my two visits to Shiraishi there was always a queue of people there, filling huge tanks with water which they claimed was health-giving. So we washed our hands, filled up our water bottles and left for new adventures.

Nichitsu Mine
日窒鉱山
1937–1970

Nichitsu Mine was challenging for us. I've been so many times to the abandoned town of Nichitsu, always passing by the mine but never daring to go in until one autumn evening with a lovely sunset.

We had to cross a dangerous bridge to access the mining area, from where we could perhaps be seen by the guards who were still around. Only a small section of the complex is actually abandoned and Nichitsu troops are everywhere.

The mine existed before World War I but serious exploitation only began when the Nichitsu Corporation bought it in 1937. The working day used to start at 8 am. Blasting would happen around 3 pm and then the shift changed. The minerals (gold, iron, zinc) were brought out by the night shift, which started at 4 pm and ended around midnight.

Today you can still see intense activity around the clock, even on weekends and holidays.

Tatsuyama Mine
竜山鉱山

Tatsuyama is a very old copper mine in Okayama. Most of the building is constructed of an awkward collection of wood which, wonderfully, has withstood the test of time.

Entering the mine was not easy and we had to climb in order to find a way in. At the top and round the back we discovered the entrance to the mine tunnel but it was full of blue water.

Inside the old skeleton of wood and metal wire we found a heaven of grass and flowers. With a little imagination this place could have been an ancient but magnificent greenhouse with a unique ecosystem roaming with forgotten species. I sincerely hope the weak and brittle structure will last a long time yet. Tatsuyama Mine was closed in 1961 and unfortunately there isn't much information about it.

The most famous copper mine in Japan, Ashio Mine in Tochigi, is also abandoned. I've visited a few times but as most of it is now demolished its history has become more interesting (though not in a positive way) than its appearance.

Matsuo Mine
松尾鉱山
1914–1969

It was a chilly 5 am in the morning when we drove towards Matsuo Mine. We left before daybreak so as not to miss the sunrise. We passed quietly through the "not yet ruined" site in the morning mist, heading towards our even quieter destination. It took us some time driving around in circles trying to figure out the best approach to the mine. And when we finally left the car, it started to rain.

The strong winter wind was howling through the eleven abandoned concrete apartment blocks with all their broken windows. These casually arranged blocks were the workers' dormitories – so many of them, like giants standing in the midst of these rugged mountains.

We trespassed into the first empty corridor, the floor was cracked and plants were creeping in everywhere. Walking through the complex took us back a hundred years – we were reliving history.

Over 4,000 workers were employed in the sulphur mine, which used to be the largest in East Asia, and the little town of Matsuo could accommodate 15,000 people. The school was also relatively big for its time, in comparison with all the tiny wooden shacks I was used to visiting.

Mine shafts

Japan's well-loved mine shafts are often maintained by the prefecture. Sometimes they even become a tourist attraction, as in these two cases.

Ponbetsu Coal Mine in Hokkaido is strikingly beautiful. Not only is it scenic, but a few of the surrounding buildings are used for art projects. But the shaft itself and the surface building are out of bounds and well guarded because the site is dangerous. The shaft, constructed in 1960, at 51 m high and 750 m deep was the largest in Asia at the time.

Another famous shaft is at Shime Coal Mine in Fukuoka prefecture, 48 m high, which was built in 1943 and abandoned in 1961. For a while, it could have been a *haikyo* but with today's flow of tourists it has become an official tourist site with its own museum, souvenir and its less delightful boundary fence. The peculiarities of this shaft brought it fame on the Reddit website where it became an *Anti-Zombie Fortress* meme.

Fuchu Military Base
米軍府中基地跡
1956–1973

Hard to imagine there could be still be an abandoned military base in Tokyo. And even more surprising when you know there are two gigantic parabolic antennas right in the middle of it – urbex magnets!

We circulated a while, but the base was well protected. There was high spiked fencing all around and no weak point in sight. The base is within a residential area where the locals are constantly looking out for trespassers. Some residences have set up tripods to help out the security services. Inevitably, there must be a fun side to catching the "bandits". A communication tower inside the complex is still in use too, therefore a guard is inside and cars go in and out.

I hesitated for some time, weighing my chances. But my fellow explorer jumped on the fence like a cat, so I followed her without a second glance behind. A short dash and we were safely hidden in the branches.

For a while we visited the buildings where a few of the athletes of the Tokyo Olympics 1964 had stayed, now covered with graffiti seemingly by two or three different artists. At the sound of a car we ran off but I came back alone a few days later.

Sometimes exploration is safer when alone, as it's easier to be careful and hide yourself. This time, I headed directly for the two antennas where the communication centre is located.

This section of the military base was part of the Communication Group of the U.S. 5th Air Force. It was active for a short period between 1956 and 1973 but made a massive contribution to U.S. Air Force communications in the early days of the Vietnam War. The two parabolic giants are 13 m high, and were part of the Japan Troposcatter System that maintained radio communication with the Misawa military base in the Tohoku region of northern Japan. Communication was made by tropospheric scatter, in which radio waves pass through the troposphere (layer of the atmosphere with an average altitude of 11 km) and some of their energy is scattered back to Earth, thus avoiding the limitations of line-of-sight systems in which the receiver can be "seen" by the transmitter. The system allowed radio communications all the way from Okinawa to Tohoku with very few terminals.

I jumped the fence again and ran to the nearest temple to catch my breath. This army base was another *haikyo* checkpoint I wanted to have in my collection.

Abandoned Dodge of Yamanashi
白沢峠の廃ダッジ
1945

This old Dodge truck somehow came to rest in the deep mountains of Shirasawa Pass, Yamanashi. It was a chilly morning, foggy, rainy. The hike was through the forest, deep and fresh. When we arrived at an elevation of 1,500 m we finally found the abandoned truck in a god-given location.

In the morning mist it looked almost holy, with the wings of an angel on a rotting body.

The Dodge WC-14 truck was brought to Japan by the U.S. army. After World War II, timber was in great demand, especially to rebuild the city of Tokyo and the neighbouring areas. This was one of the trucks used to carry the wood from the mountain villages to the plains of Kanto. Unsurprisingly it got stuck one day.

I came back three years later during the winter to find the Dodge unchanged. Still just as amazing when surrounded by snow. I hope the atmosphere of the place comes across well on the photos because the scene is, in reality, simply breathtaking.

Negishi Grandstand
A monument of Joy and War

横浜旧根岸競馬場
1866–1983

In the middle of a neighbourhood of Yokohama, not far from Tokyo, proudly stands one of Japan's most famous ruins: Negishi Grandstand. In 1866, the Meiji emperor ordered the construction of a racecourse and an English architect was commissioned to build this grandstand. The Great Kanto earthquake of 1923 destroyed most of Tokyo and Yokohama but the grandstand survived. A few years later, in 1929, it was rebuilt by J.H. Morgan using techniques designed to withstand earthquakes. The building was often visited by the emperor himself and even more regularly by his successor, Hirohito.

This building is famous as a *haikyo*, not only for its impressive architecture but also as an impenetrable fortress. Located between the United States Fleet Activities Yokosuka and the Park of Negishi, it's monitored by surveillance cameras. As if that wasn't enough, it's also surrounded by a barbed-wire fence, curved inward to inflict damage on potential intruders. Negishi Grandstand seemed like an impossible *haikyo* until a fellow explorer suggested I should follow him.

One winter's day we meet at 5 am in front of the building. It's completely dark but I'm thrilled to be about to discover the secret entrance of this place.

My friend is obviously just as excited and he's travelled a long way, driving all night for this. Despite his quiet and serious air, in no time he's climbed up the fence like a ninja barely touching the barbed wire and landed very nimbly on the other side. I really don't want to disappoint him and try my best to execute the same stunt. Without thinking I jump, trying to reach the top and avoid the barbed area, concentrating on the landing. And here I am, on the other side, with a few cuts to my hands.

We run to the first door – locked. We hide a moment then make another run, another little climb, another run and finally reach an entrance. Majestic as this place is, we're asking for trouble. I wish I'd asked for some kind of authorization but too late now. We go into the grandstand. It's cold and plunged in darkness. Water drips into big puddles from pipes in the high ceiling, echoing loudly.

We take the stairs to the third floor, where most of the action used to take place in the quartermaster's office, the administrative offices and various other rooms. All signs written in English in the same lettering as at Fuchu Military Base. And there's more: the commandant's office, a briefing room, and then another room that seems to have been a military radio communications centre.

The sun is rising fast. As the first rays penetrate we hear voices on all sides. Old folk out with their dogs; teenagers having fun on the basketball court; U.S. Army soldiers joking and laughing loudly outside; kids playing in the park, happily enjoying the background music.

And here we are, in the midst of all this turmoil, hidden.

We look around to see the natural colours of the building for the first time. It looks like a big rusty shed and the only objects I can find are big old lightbulbs. It seems there was a bowling alley here at one point so these could be more recent relics.

We finally arrive on the seventh floor. There are actually three of these, one in each of the three towers. Then an eighth floor connected by a ladder, probably leading to a ventilator on the roof, secured with a large padlock and chain. My friend winks at me: *We'll go there later, at sunset. It's not safe now.* I'll go along with that.

Back to 1942 and World War II. Horse racing was prohibited. The Japanese military decided to use this building for printing (fake notes for propaganda reasons) and the stable was converted into a prison for Australian detainees. In 1945, the U.S. military took over. General MacArthur himself discovered the printing machines and made use of them. 140,000 acts of capitulation were printed here and distributed throughout Japan. Two years later, the U.S. military claimed the entire complex, built a residential area known as Area X, now Negishi Heights, and the grandstand was used as administrative offices.

Today, the building no longer belongs to the U.S. military: in 1983, the whole territory of Negishi Heights was returned to Japan. The grandstand was abandoned, protected by a simple barrier, then a fence, and finally this unyielding barbed wire.

After spending hours taking photos, time suddenly stands still and the cold slowly penetrates me. I try to stay close to a sunlit window, but it makes little difference. I glance at my watch constantly, wondering when we'll finally get out. I can still hear the voices outside, but finally sunset arrives. My friend takes out his tools and half an hour later, clang! The hatch door opens. We climb onto the deck and stay there a long time, gazing at the buildings in Yokohama, the bay and the factories – a really unique view. Fewer people are around, some walking their dogs and others jogging, but the military base seems more or less asleep…

We have to go. My ninja friend takes care of everything, locking the padlock, closing the doors, as if we'd never been here. We're now outside the building, hidden near the entrance.

I go first, moving slowly under the surveillance camera, approaching the barbed wire. I try to pull myself up to a small space between the fence and barbed wire where I can get through. Then slash! My hands are scratched. The blood rushes to my head, my heart pounds. I don't know how but I crawl over and hang on the other side, trapped by the legs. An old lady stands there, watching me, bewildered. I must look like a wounded burglar. I hear myself asking desperately: *Can you help me?* That scares her and she hurries away. I finally fall to the ground, covered with blood. But there's no time to lose, we have to go. My friend tosses the bags over the fence, then jumps back to my side with amazing ease. Of course he has the right gear but still I feel there's more to him than he admits.

We drive to a local pharmacy to find something to disinfect my wounds. Astonished, the pharmacist asks me what happened. I answer simply: *Fixed my car*, and leave the store with ripped jeans half-dragging on the floor. Once cleaned up, I shake hands with my friend. I'll never forget the good part of this adventure, and it's all thanks to him.

Gunkanjima

The Abandoned Battleship Island

軍艦島
1890–1974

Hashima, better known as Gunkanjima – Battleship Island – because it looks like a military warship, hides a completely abandoned city behind its huge sea wall.

Coal was discovered on Hashima in 1810, but it was only in 1890, when Mitsubishi bought the island, that mining began in earnest. Workers moved to the island with their families and by 1959 Hashima was a working city, with 5,300 residents and the highest population density in the world. The island was completely covered with apartment blocks, schools, hospital, gym, cinema, shops, shrine, pachinko parlor, bath houses, bars, even a brothel.

The mine closed in 1974 – petroleum had become cheaper and easier to produce – and the island was abandoned until the 2000s, when it was photographed, used in music videos and even appeared in movies. In 2009, the city of Nagasaki set up an official tour, allowing visitors to see a small portion of the island.

立入禁止
長崎市

It was around this time that I decided to visit the *other side* of the island. Since then, I've been back a few times. This time, we'll be accompanied by Doutoku Sakamoto. He's an official guide and head of the association that wants Gunkanjima to be designated as a UNESCO World Heritage site. Sakamoto was born on the island in 1954.

It's 6 am when we board the little boat. As soon as we leave the coast, the captain shuts down the lights. We cannot be seen going to the island. Excitement grows as we recognize the shape of Gunkanjima, even darker than the night.

We reach a section of the seawall where there is a flight of steps, and the captain tells us to jump quickly from the bow. He'll be back at the time agreed; we'll wait for him behind the wall. After climbing the ladder next to the No Entry sign, we jump down. We're here!

During my first trip I didn't know where to begin. I just knew we could get around very quickly, as a former miner had said that crossing the island took less time than smoking a cigarette. In the end, I saw most of it in an hour.

The first building we go into, the school, constructed in 1958, was one of the most recent. Typhoons have seriously damaged it and exposed the foundations. The school is built on an artificial section of the island and we can see the water just below. At high tide the school basement fills with water.

At the entrance we're welcomed by a wicked clown-tiger painted on the wall.

Upstairs, the rooms are full of light and the atmosphere is magical. We can almost hear the students singing along to the little piano as the wind whistles through the wide-open windows. On the blackboard in the staff room, previous explorers have left their signatures.

I spent a night in this school a few years back. A candle was lit in the old glass bulb. My friends and I shared chocolate, a little alcohol, and many stories before finally falling asleep, while fighting against the humid wind and coldness. I am sure the ghosts remember us. A wave breaks on the concrete walls and wakes me from my dreamy thoughts.

Sakamoto-san recalls: "I'll always remember our science teacher, Hikawa-sensei. We nicknamed him "The Turtle", *Kame-chan*. He was around 50 and his classroom was filled with laughter. There was always some giggling and whispering at the start of each lesson: our teacher never zipped up his fly properly after going to the restroom. His embarrassed smile was so touching."

The school was officially closed on 31 March 1974.

Nearby is Block 65 (65棟), one of the most impressive buildings on the island. A digital version of it is featured in the James Bond movie *Skyfall*. This U-shaped building, nine storeys high, is seriously decayed. The concrete was mixed with seawater, so the salt and humidity have corroded the framework – the steel turns to dust when touched.

The first seven floors on the left were built in 1945, the only building constructed in Japan that year. In 1947 another two floors were added, and two years later the central section was built. Finally, in 1953, they added the building on the right and named it *The New 65*. It had nice apartments and even flush toilets.

There are 317 apartments in Block 65. We glance quickly into each, looking for something interesting. They all seem pretty similar, with tatami mats, sometimes in surprisingly good condition. There was very little privacy. Sakamoto-san mentions that he sometimes spotted his girlfriend on the other side of the building.

Sakamoto-san: "Roofs were important in Hashima. They were used for all sorts of unexpected things. Some of them were covered with antennas. Another one had its own bench and even a swing. In the summer, at night, lots of people met up there. School students, grandfathers and grandmothers … and the strumming of guitars. It was comforting knowing there was always someone overhead. And being up there gave us a sense of freedom."

Between the stairs we find an old Kyoraku pachinko machine. It looks very simple, a bit smaller than those you find in modern pachinko parlors.

We can find a lot of old objects here, whereas there's almost nothing in the other buildings. It was occupied until the very end. People probably had to leave things behind.

Right next to Block 65 stands the hospital, built in 1958 but not the first hospital on the island. The previous one burned down. Wooden shacks never lasted long in such a crowded place.

The first floor houses the doctor's offices, the X-ray room and the surgery; there's an old coloured light lying on the floor. The second floor has the wards for the patients. The staff lived on the top floor. From most of the rooms up here you can see the school playground, which must have been comforting for the sick.

Sakamoto-san: "Once, I even saw some snow. I believe it was during my first year of junior high school. My memory is vague but I remember an intense cold that hit the island and we even managed to build a snowman in front of the school building. It was the only time I saw snow on Hashima."

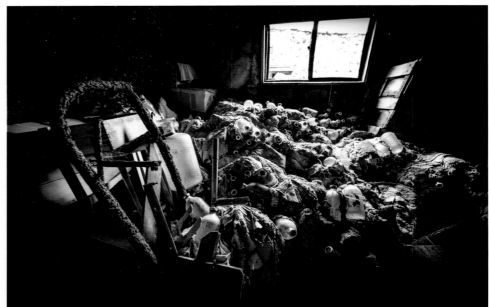

We are now in Hashima Ginza, where the wives went to shop, where the husbands went after work for drinks. The buildings crowd in and bridges pass overhead. On a rainy day you wouldn't need an umbrella.

In the distance, there's something odd. This is the famous Hell's Staircase (地獄段), often called the Stairway to Hell in homage to Led Zeppelin. The kids used to play around here all the time.

The Hashima Shrine is at the top of those stairs, and the view is fantastic. You can see the four large apartment blocks (Blocks 16, 17, 18 and 19) with their roof gardens. We'll walk through those buildings as we go back down.

Little by little, the sun is starting to set.

The shrine is very plain now although it used to be much bigger. The first version caught fire in 1935 and a new one was built the following year. It is the dwelling-place of two gods: Oyamazumi, the Guardian of the Mine, and Konpira, the God of the Sea. Every spring there was a festival (*matsuri*) known as Yamagami-sai. The locals paraded round the island carrying the portable shrine (*mikoshi*), starting from the Stairway to Hell.

We're now passing through Blocks 16, 17, 18 and 19. Three of them were built in 1918 and the last added in 1921: they're much older than Block 65. Overgrown as they are, these buildings are the most scenic location on the island.

Sakamoto-san: "Most of the islanders were miners living in two-room apartments, from 63 to 112 square metres. For a family of five it might seem a little cramped now, but back in the day it was really just a matter of organization. All the apartments had the exact same design but we managed to give each of them its own particular style. The islanders have fond memories of their old homes. They were easy to live in and everyone got along well."

The rooms were allocated on a points system. Points were granted according to the status of each worker and the type and size of their family. With those points, people were able to move to better apartments (often closer to the toilets) or even to Block 65.

Sakamoto-san: "Before I moved to Block 65 I was living in Block 16–17. There, everyone shared the same bathroom. It was so dark that we had to switch the light on even during the day. I was particularly afraid of going there at night so every time we changed apartments I prayed my heart out that we would finally end up near the bathroom. I was lucky to finally move to Block 65. And by the end of Hashima, I even had the honour of living in an apartment with its own private bathroom. It's funny to think about it now, but at the time, it was like a dream to me to have my own bathroom."

As the sun sets the apartment blocks are really interesting to watch, as the rays strike through the many breaches in the wall.

Sakamoto-san: "The north wind is very strong in February and every day people watched the rough seas. During this season there weren't many boats. Even the itinerant tradesmen from Takahama didn't come any more. Fewer supplies, less fresh fruit and vegetables. Winters were very harsh."

After drinking sake and watching the sunset, we walk towards Block 30, the last building on the itinerary. Dating from 1916, this was the first reinforced concrete building in Japan. It looks like a perfect little cube but the steps are all falling to pieces and it's too dangerous to climb up.

Night has come and the stars are shining. Here, at the heart of the island, we can relax and enjoy the show, listening to the never-ending song of the waves crashing on the seawall. We don't want this romantic moment to end but we must carry on. Taking photos at night needs more time, especially on Gunkanjima.

We leave the city to scout the area around the mine. Mitsubishi demolished it when the island was abandoned, and there isn't much left. The galleries are probably still there, running deep under the sea.

Access was by elevator and the miners had to be patient about reaching their workplaces. The coalface was up to a kilometre underground in temperatures of 45 °C, the miners pressed against each other, crouching most of the time. Gas explosions and tunnel collapses were thought normal. There were four or five deaths each month. However, the decent wages attracted many workers to the island.

Not everyone came here for the money though. Gunkanjima has a much darker side: Korean prisoners from World War II lived in the buildings along the southern wall of the island, seven or eight of them in each tiny room. Separated from their families and wives (most of whom became sex slaves), some mutilated themselves in order to escape the island, some swam to the next island, others simply committed suicide by jumping out of a window. Most died of malnutrition, *karoshi* (death from overwork) and other illnesses or accidents in the mine. Of the 500 Koreans working on the island between 1939 and 1945, 120 died there.

The Japanese miners seem to have had happier lives. After work, they went to the communal bath. Then they'd go for drinks in the Ginza-Hashima district, near by Block 65.

Sakamoto-san: "The island was never pitch black, not even in the middle of the night. The mines never stopped. The lights were always on in the homes of those who were working. When the first shift was over, a second set of windows would light up. And so on with the third and fourth shifts. The light travelled from one window to the next. With this constant light we felt reassured, especially when we came back by boat from the mainland late at night."

The day the workers heard the mine was closing, they hung their heads in shock and sadness. Then they gathered a few belongings and left the rest behind, hoping that one day it would reopen.

Imagine, on a full moon like tonight, the miners talking loudly in the steamy bath, singing in the bars, talking to the ladies in the back street and playing pachinko. The Hashima-Ginza is all lit up, a few kids still running around. Block 65, full of warm orange light, with wives calling from the balcony, telling their men to come home for dinner. Young miners enjoying sake, going to meet their friends, some of them up on the rooftops. In the background, the constant buzz from the mines.

Sakamoto-san: "After the bath, I was always impatient to buy a fruit juice at the Nomo grocery store. There was a little girl we called Nomo's Kayo-chan. Everyone loved her and she was like a little celebrity. She always smiled at me and had a way about her that made us stay at the store so long we'd end up catching a cold right after our bath. I still see Kayo-chan riding around in her motorized wheelchair. And since nobody knows her real age she'll always be Nomo's Kayo-chan."

We keep walking. It'll be dawn soon. Finally, in the morning mist, we recognize the light of the boat crossing the waves.

Sakamoto-san: "For those of us who lived on the island, it still is… our *furusato* (hometown). It's where we come from."

The 70-year-old bell rings continuously on the approach to the pier. We jump aboard and the captain asks us to hide. He'll take us back to everyday life.

The last resident left the island on 20 April 1974.

Thanks to:

The *haikyo explorers* I had the pleasure to travel with.

Junya-kun, for all those fun trips and adventures we shared.

The **Haikyo Deflation Spiral** and **Michael John Grist** websites that got me started.

Toto. I can drive thousand of kilometres listening to my favourite band without falling asleep.

May and **Jing**, my past girlfriends, who pushed me out of my comfort zone and explored haikyo with me.

Sakamoto-san for the fantastic afternoon walk on Gunkanjima.

The Jonglez Team for this book including Thomas, Stéphanie and Caroline with whom I had the pleasure to work.

My many correctors, **Mitch**, **Elijah**, **Stéphanie**, **Gene**, **Amaury**.

Risa, my extremely sweet wife, always there for me.

My **lovely family**, many of you know how amazing you are and how derelict I am in comparison!

Last but not least, **my followers** who never fail to motivate me.

For more adventures, check my own websites **Totoro Times** and **Haikyo.org**

A few more foreign *haikyoists* also publish very interesting articles online, such as **Tokyo Times**, **Gakuran** and **Abandoned Kansai**.

All photographs by **Jordy Meow**

Design: **Stéphanie Benoit**
Editing: **Caroline Lawrence**
Proof-reading: **Kimberly Bess**

© **JONGLEZ 2015**
Registration of copyright: October 2015 – Edition: 01
ISBN: 978-2-36195-132-0
Printed in China by Leo Press